PASSP

My full name

....

....

Birthday

....

....

Birthplace

....

....

Eye color

....

....

Hair color

....

....

My state of mind
(as I write this)

....

....

Best feature

....

....

Quirk (s)

....

....

Signature

....

....

Published by Page 90 Publishing
220 S. Cedros Avenue
Solana Beach,
CA 92075 USA
Page-90.com

ISBN(s)
978-0-9996375-2-4 Paperback edition
978-0-9996375-3-1 Hardcover edition

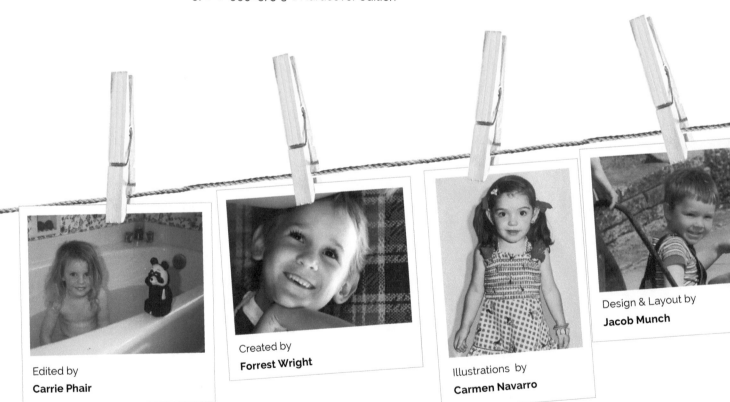

Edited by
Carrie Phair

Created by
Forrest Wright

Illustrations by
Carmen Navarro

Design & Layout by
Jacob Munch

why this book...

A long time ago I accidentally interviewed my grandmother, Meme, over a lunch at a restaurant called Clyde's in Columbia, Maryland. This is when I found out that she had always wanted to be a private investigator, that she had changed her legal name illegally, and that she had grown up in a house with dirt floors. Each of these revelations created tangents in our conversation and before I knew it, we had chatted for three hours. Things that had never made sense to me about her, or memories with her, suddenly did. I discovered greater empathy for Meme once I knew her struggles. And, best of all, I felt like I knew her as a person, not just my grandmother. The idea for this book was born out of that conversation. **Thank you, Meme.**

25 years later, while writing this, my sister-in-law's sister Elena became terminally ill. Elena and I are the Godparents to our niece Rio. The day Elena agreed to go into hospice is the day I understood how very important it is for us to share who we really are with the younger people in our lives. It was my intention to get this book to her as soon as possible so she could tell her story and leave it with Rio or, perhaps, her daughter Aliyah. Unfortunately, Elena passed away the very next day so we will never know her answers to these questions.
Elena, thank you for putting a fire under my butt to get this book published.

My fabulous friend Samantha Martin had the very good idea to crowdsource some of the questions in this book. Fortunately, our friends are very smart and creative and they contributed readily. **Friends like Josh Uranga, Tess Price, Nick Sing, Josie Jackson, Lauren Turton, Olive Primo, Phil Walters, Wendy Melnick and Claire Fulton.**

And, finally, a thank you to my "editor" Carrie who won't take credit as a co-creator of this book but who has had a very big hand in its creation. She's made the questions better, brought structure to the madness, and helped this move from concept to creation.
Thank you, Carrie, for helping me realize a dream.

Dear Author,

This book is not for everyone to write. It's for you to share more of who you really are with someone in your life.

This is about the transfer of stories and wisdom from one generation to another.

This is your chance to reveal more of your truths. Some of the topics here are light and fun. Some are serious. Kids can handle it. They want to know you and they want to know the truth. They are very smart, and they want to be addressed as people, not children. Still, it's up to you to balance honesty with tact, transparency with appropriateness. Only you know what's right.

If you fill out a few questions every few days, you'll be done in no time. Do not worry about your handwriting.
It's time to tell your story.

Dear Reader,

This book is not for everyone to read.
It's especially for you.

I am giving you this book because _____

_____

_____

_____

_____

_____

Chapter 1

groW

When I was a child, I lived in

What made it special was

I remember meeting you at

My first impression was

I **loved** eating

But I hated when I had to eat

o avoid eating
omething I would

A meal I'd love to
share with you is

One of my favorite childhood memories is

It would be **so fun** if we had the **tradition** of

The one thing (toy, clothes, gift, etc.)
**I always wanted as a kid
but never got** was

Something from my childhood
that **I would love to pass
on to you** is

One of my **favorite games** to play was

It would be really fun if the **two of us** **could play**

BINGO

11	56	24	19	34	76
45	34	78	99	14	23
58	91	31	40	55	83
09	45	78	12	62	39
45	67	71	90	64	80
14	52	48	91		

If I got **into trouble as a kid** it was most likely because

If you were to
get a time out,
I'd imagine it was
because

MY BIGGEST

FEAR

WAS

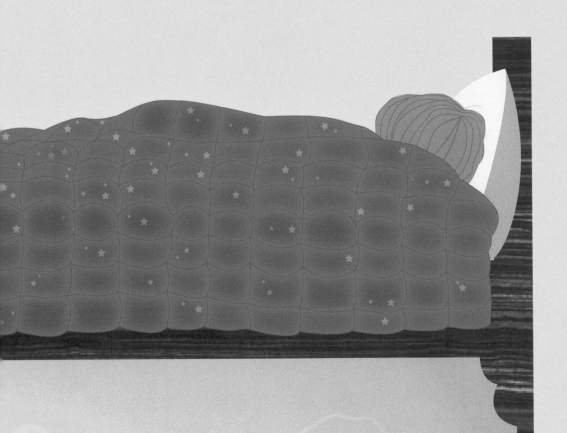

IF YOU GET SCARED
YOU CAN

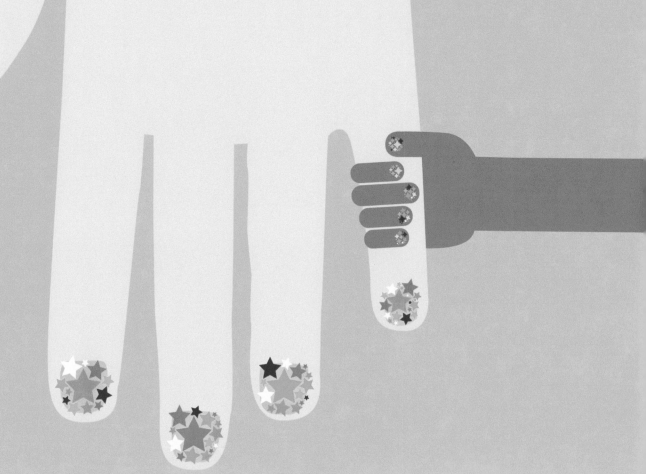

One of **my favorite people** growing up was

We spent **our time**

hope you have
**someone in
your life who**

My friends
would have awarded me
MOST LIKELY TO

I award you
MOST LIKELY TO

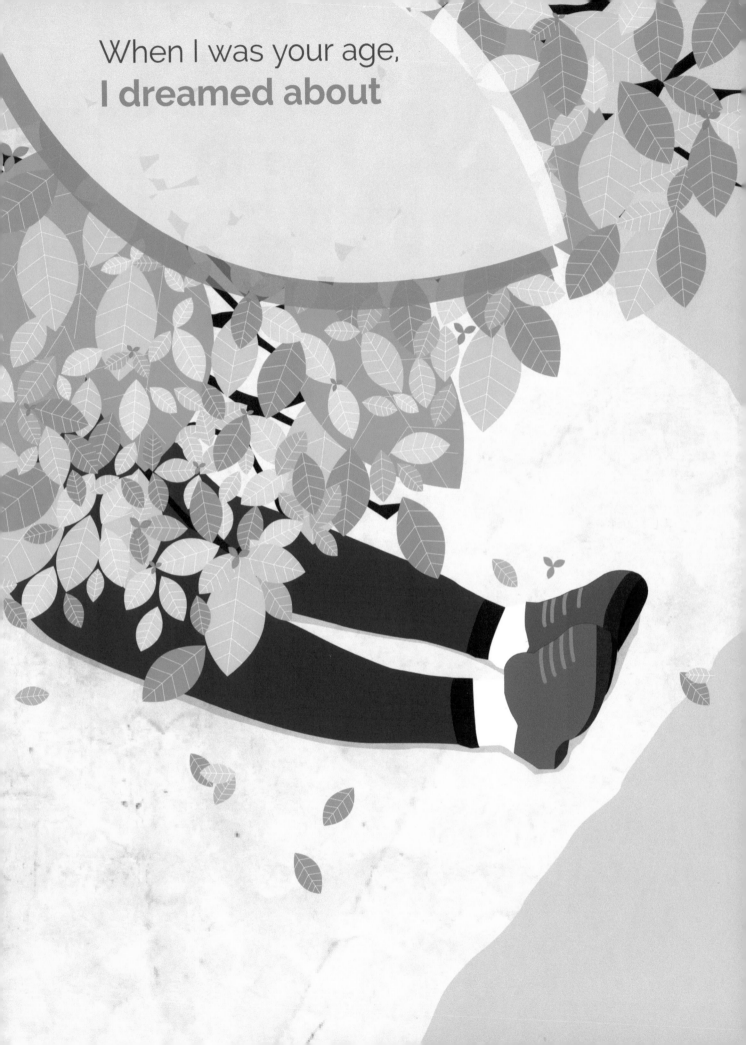

When I was your age,
I dreamed about

Chapter 2

growing old

Life is not a straight line. In my lifetime I've been

I see **you doing**
things like

A picture is worth a thousand words.

This is how I see myself.

(It's up to you. Draw a self-portrait or place a photograph here.)

And this is

how I see you.

(Draw your reader or paste your favorite picture of them here.)

I try to help
others by

I challenge
you to **GO ON
AN ADVENTURE
ONE DAY** that
incorporates
these three things:

(1)

(2)

(3)

My best friend as an adult is

We met

They make me feel

One of our **favorite things to do together is**

In a friend,

look for these traits:

I've fallen in love before and I knew it was love because

I had my heart broken when

The thing I want to tell you about love is

Every person and every family
has secrets.
This is one I want to tell you.

I'm telling you
this secret because

These are all the places I've traveled to
(Mark them on the map or write them out however you want)

I remember going to these places with you

I would love to go with you to

I'm proud
of a time when I

I'm **proud
of you** for

These are
3 things I have not yet done
and I really wish I had:

These are
3 things I would like you and I to do together:

Chapter 3

grow together

ing

The **best advice** I ever
received was from

They said

Here's something I hope you **take to heart**

If I could give everyone on the planet
ONE THING, it would be

The
one trait
I wish I
could
pass on
to you is

In my imagination, you think these things about me

Here are the words I use to describe you:

MY POWER WOULD BE   MY MISSION WOULD BE

BUT EVERY HERO HAS THEIR WEAKNESSES AND CHALLENGES.
IN MY LIFE I HAVE STRUGGLED WITH

I GRANT YOU THIS SUPERPOWER

I would like to be remembered for

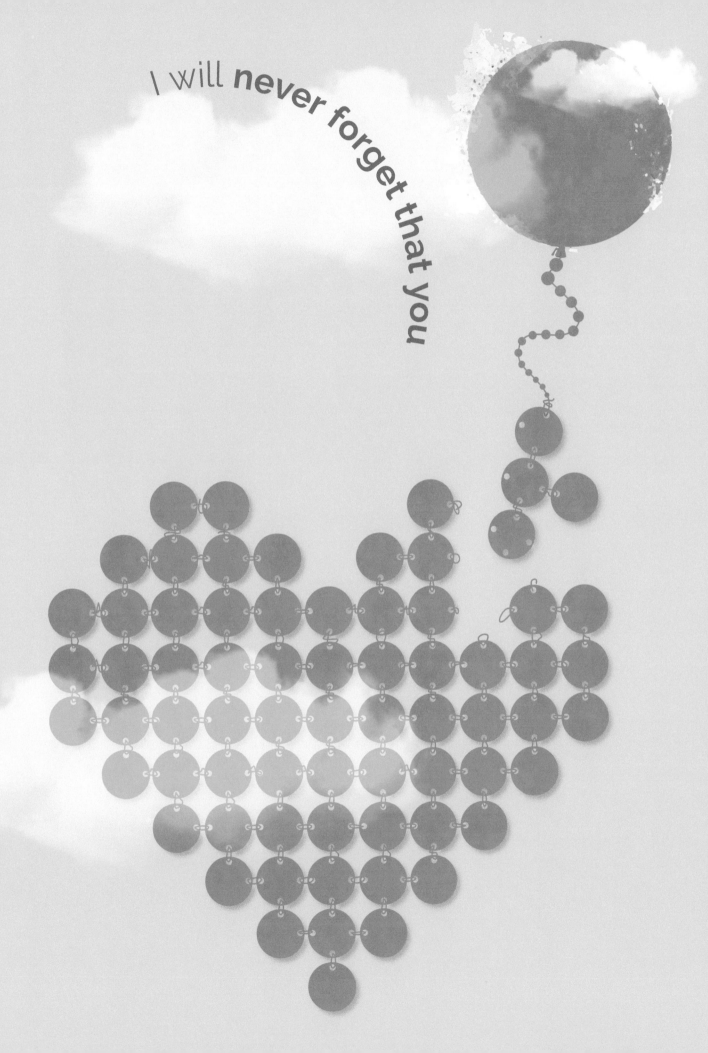

This photo sums up what
makes life so special.

Thanks for being part of my life

"Aging is an extraordinary process where you become the person you always should have been."

DAVID BOWIE

CPSIA information can be obtained
at www.ICGtesting.com
Printed in the USA
LVHW070610100222
710635LV00002B/6

9 780999 637531